To the Sound

*For Steve,
With gratitude —
Vivian*

poems by

Vivian Eyre

Finishing Line Press
Georgetown, Kentucky

To the Sound

Copyright © 2013 by Vivian Eyre
ISBN 978-1-62229-428-2 First Edition
All rights reserved under International and Pan-American Copyright Conventions. No part of this book may be reproduced in any manner whatsoever without written permission from the publisher, except in the case of brief quotations embodied in critical articles and reviews.

ACKNOWLEDGMENTS

With gratitude for the wisdom and encouragement of Jim Moore and Juliet Patterson. With thanks to the editors of the journals in which these poems first appeared; some with different titles, some in different forms.

Asheville Poetry Review	"The Visits"
Bellingham Review	"Carry the Body into Light"
FRiGG online	"Late Interiors"
	"My Father's Sketchbook"
	"Paper Napkins"
	"Spaghetti"
	"What Follows"
Green Hills Literary Lantern	"Arrangements"
Limestone: Art, Prose, Poetry	"Empty Teacup"
	"Red Fishing Net"
Oberon Magazine	"September"
Permafrost	"Summer Letter"
Sanskrit	"Before the Amen"
Spoon River Poetry Review	"Tender Trading"
The Chaffin Journal	"Window Fishing"
The Griffin	"To the Sound"

Editor: Christen Kincaid
Cover Photo: Patrick Haggerty
Author Photo: Karen Mortimore
Cover Design: Elizabeth Maines

Printed in the USA on acid-free paper.
Order online: www.finishinglinepress.com
also available on amazon.com

Author inquiries and mail orders:
Finishing Line Press
P. O. Box 1626
Georgetown, Kentucky 40324
U. S. A.

TABLE OF CONTENTS

3	The Visits
4	Carry the Body into Light
5	Before the Amen
6	Red Fishing Net
7	Summer Letter
8	Twilight Bridge
9	Empty Teacup
10	Funeral Parlor
11	Arrangements
12	Late Interiors
13	September
14	Spaghetti
15	Window Fishing
16	Paper Napkins
17	Paper Napkins II
18	My Father's Sketchbook
19	What Follows
20	The Gift
21	Snow Falls
22	Tender Trading
23	Pipes Cove
24	To the Sound

for my sister always

The Visits

I place a penny in your open palm:
a hummingbird weighs less than this.

You want to die in sleep like your husband,
not like your sister, naked on a kitchen floor.

After I die, eat biscotti, drink cocoa, you say.
Chocolate, like sorrow, melts on the tongue.

Have you ever seen hummingbird eggs?
I hand you two pearls of barley.

A hummingbird's bed is a weave of webs
and lichen and grows as the hummingbird grows.

A doctor's card nests in your hands, rosary beads
in your lap, lap blanket as gorget. After the visit,

you never answer the phone. Never
want to shower. On the side table, irises

and chamomile tea. Imagine a sea of wings.
You vanish inside yourself, foot falls off

wheelchair's rest, the step of a weary inn.
Now you sit by the window,

your trembling eyelids like a black-chinned flybird.
You ask me: *How does a hummingbird die?*

Carry the Body into Light

On the solarium window, a sticker captivates a patient.
Paper beads pool. That same window overlooks

a low tangle of *Rosa rugosa*. Mockingbird guards red bitter.
Doused by sprinklers, cat curls into a small firm ball. Door open—

A child plays with a ball of electrical wire. In a mother's confusion
she places a raw meatball into her mouth instead of a sip of Stoli.

I brush crumbs off grandmother's blouse. She tells me how
bumblebees come from spiders and tigers. Says I laugh

like her granddaughter. Here, nothing cries,
a woman says.   No one cares in which room she invites

Cervantes to write. Black locusts entice lightning
to extinguish itself. Rake dry leaves in the dark,

plant verbena by porch light, I wonder if
verbena bewitches butterflies,

if my spade were flat, if loneliness rolls off.
In Spain, Don Diego dies.

No one is there to open the curtains.
No one carries his body into light.

Before the Amen

Imperfect hands, fingertips listing in different directions,
clutching a locket, oval-shaped. Inside petals
that fell from the altar of St. Therese in Rome.

In the grotto where Rose once knelt,
her well-lined thumb traces the sign—forehead, lips, chest.
Gazing into the saint's ewe eyes,

Before the ibex climbs mountains, I heard her say,
he must cross rivers. Or was it: *Why*

must I forgive the same crowd over
and over?

Red Fishing Net

1
What are you looking for?
Anything. He's up to his ankles in bay.
In a figure eight killies swim. Glimmering silver
transforms him so utterly. Beyond threshold,
Anything isn't found—even though the light is enormous.

2
Rose says: When you pray, be specific or else
He won't know what you want. Before raisin toast,
Everything happens. Four hundred and ninety-nine questions
in Father Kinkead's catechism. Rose sifts:
how to enter The Gates (if there are Gates)?
Wheeled to the window, she sinks
between paper-green covers, not far from sand and sky.

3
His net stabs water—a gap in knotted string—
enough daylight remains. Pail and sieve
above the high-water mark.
Sand can be a savior.
Anything can be found easily in sand.

Summer Letter

You were the only one
who wrote me that summer on Peconic Bay
where every night but Sunday
girls stood in line for letters with Palmer script,
where I stood on a porch long after
the first letter of my last name passed.

On the day I held my breath
long enough to float the dead man's float,
I dragged my finger under your sealed envelope,
the single page folded twice, eight words
in Garbo's loopy script.

You're an endless letter in cursive,
so much harder to read than print.
              I never told you
I traded your silver cross for
a rabbit's foot.

Twilight Bridge
> *Most of what matters in the world*
> *takes place in our absence.*
> —Salman Rushdie

When Beijing fell, brushstrokes blossomed
under Yellow Mountain's glow,
under seas of clouds, mists circling. Pines
rooted in rock. Oh, those crooked pines.

No one remembers Zhu Sheng in his straw hat,
painting ancient gentlemen, three hundred years
in *The Mustard-seed Garden*—orchid, bamboo.

At the twilight bridge,
twigs break in a needle beak,
hummingbird's nest a nut-sized cup.

My palms, a kingdom, blanketing my eyes
        foot over wing
        above a line of violet—

Empty Teacup
after Bonnard's Breakfast Room

Your hand wants to touch the delft.
Porcelain constellations
so orderly on snowy ground.
Shrunken in white garments, women
in cadmium halos, caps like cupolas on an ancient church.
In a room set from above clouds,
women melt into the next moment
as the chair melds into the window frame.

Late in life, Bonnard painted
sixty dining room scenes. I inhabit
the women disobeying spatial rules. Women
with backpacks of family lore—
as a spine straightens under story's weight. Who said:
> *Men inherit land.*
> *Women inherit people.*

The curator insists: Bonnard
was no story-painter. No message in lavish arrangements:
burnished pitcher, brioche, eggplant-shaded plums.

Behind shape-color-shadow,
I wonder Bonnard's relief. A doorway is still a doorway—
an imprecise measure of departure.

Funeral Parlor

In this room, the lamp shade maps the world's great seas.
Framed nautical knots. Lemon-scented laminate. *The Room,*
that's what people dread most—the walking into,
          the funeral director says,
opens a leather-bound book: *Metal or Wood?*
In a tufted chair is where the wind kicks-up,
offs his glasses, like an offing after friends,
after making their arrangements. Relief is sailing to Saints
                              Thomas & Kitts
like the invisible lines between islands. Cornering a bookshelf,
a bottled vessel, the agony of sails so full up.

On this foreign shore, escape is my parked car—
sonnet remembrance wind chimes—
salt of the undertaken like stains on a crumpled list.
A checkmark is my knock on Rose's door.

Arrangements

I remember Rose's Ozone Park kitchen,
the portable suitcase Victrola played Ferrante & Teicher.
Julliard prodigies. Concert halls in ball parks
before they became the movie theme twins.

Our first arrangement, *Moon River*.
With her chair angled like a twin piano,
Rose sang over my wrong chords, played in arpeggio.

Who could forget her fondness for yellow: embroidery, twinsets, cars,
how important "just so" was, her famous peach kuchen,
how she lingered over *going*—
        as in: *wherever you're going . . .*
        I'm going . . . your way. Moon River.

Late Interiors

How many stars align
as postage stamps
affixed to a swath of night?
Decipherable night
siphoning through.
Nothing needs doing,
no need for oars.
Everything arranged
by interior light.

September

Sadness sits in the midst of town
where streets press together like fingertips

and masons break mortar walls along Hylow's brook
where Mary's hand arches a graveyard gate

where wastes of roses frame a gabled house,
its only window shuttered.

My father with half-tanned arms sits
at the kitchen table. His fingers holding fried dough,

dusted with powdered sugar, hand frozen mid-air,
cheeks puffed out like a blowfish on the dock.

Hunger drove him to those zeppoles,
grease and sweet brought back

Bensonhurst. Every September,
I close my eyes to see his face more clearly,

leaves rustling like crinoline,
those burning leaves, the smell of cinnamon.

Spaghetti

My father never learned to twirl spaghetti
without a spoon. On boyhood Sundays
before zeppoles San Giuseppe, before baseball,

he'd twist his fork left —then right
like his favorite switch-hitter. Noodles in the strike zone
as long as that fork touched the plate. The lift

like swinging at a screwball.
Be a man, his father said, holding up a masterpiece
of noodles twined round his fork.

Confirmation Day, my father hit a homer up Joralemon
in Mantle's Number 7 baseball shirt.
That night at Napoli's, he saw the ball player

behind a mound of spaghetti. My wide-eyed father,
with paper napkin and waiter's pencil,
waiting for an autograph as Mantle put down

his spoon. Not before another season
would that boy measure himself
in the smooth, in the prong.

Window Fishing

August rain. Red snapper hooked through the eye.
Window fishing from a fin-tailed Buick.

With baloney, he'd bait one shank hook—
once. Father's fishing rules for girls. In the backseat,

my bamboo pole bound with electrical tape
and assorted weights: slammers, zappers,

sprites or was it stripes? When his head bobbed
into sleep, I snuck away to scout flat stones.

At the skimming tournament,
he'd throw out the bait:

Do you know what Russians call skipping stones?
Baking pancakes, for the circles they make.

My summer education—
how I'd cover a rag over the snapper's head,

blindly work out the hook.

Paper Napkins

The night of the Clay-Liston fight,
I tuned in the Emerson,
my father's fingers too thick to fit the dials.

The Louisiana Lip
was our boxer. With each circular dance,
we'd hoot above the static.

The other featured bout—
Bedtime on a School Night,
before the final bell.

Next morning at the kitchen table:
a boxing portrait on a paper napkin.

I don't know when my father learned to sketch
unless I count the Correspondence School for Famous Artists,
or the plastic mask on our television's face,

not too opaque to trace. The white napkin:
victor's arm raised-up, wishbone legs,
the loser flattened over *CLAY*.

After that match any paper napkin was his canvas.
No smudgy ballpoint words. Father's point-of-view:
the world a triumph of circles, arrows, squares.

Paper Napkins II

Borrowing the waitress's pencil, my sister draws
on a paper napkin: a circle around a broken square
and labels it *ME*. After his memorial,
napkin portraits mount up.

My sister, same age as Clay when he won,
wonders how I know that. Under the window's reversed
gold lettering, I confess the paper napkin story plus

how I tossed Dad's canvas squarely over breakfast remains,
how blame is a ring of coffee grinds.

Two drained glasses of Chablis,
and my sister says she forgives me,
while her hand hovers over her napkin's face.

I wonder if forgiveness follows rules like boxing matches:
weight and weigh-in, phantom punches,
knockdown-knockout-count.

My Father's Sketchbook

Hiroshige travel portrait taped to the inside cover
of my father's sketchbook. In full kimono, Wisteria Maid
stands alone at a transfer station holding a wild flag,

wisteria branch. Odd pairing.
Father's neat straight lines, numbers running
along the sides for roadwork, molten earth of another planet.

On the next page, he drew a mast,
long racemes tethered to a sailboat,
wisteria petals on a paper wave.

In high school, I taped
Wisteria Maid to my bedroom wall,
a rendering became my doorway.

After I left, he must have rescued that maid,
with her hand hidden in a hem of intricate knots.
What hides can be hidden in a sketchbook.

My father's sketch with a No. 2 pencil:
      no hint of woman,
           wisteria petals recklessly floating downstream.

What Follows

There's nothing in this city to remind me:
no Yankee games, bait shops, no homemade ragu.

Brilliant sun for the first time in months.
Blood pulses enough for a jog down Commonwealth

into kites of pollen. Coughing tightens the string.
Winded bleary, I collapse on the curb alone, except

for a man smoking a *guinea-stinker*,
my father used to say, after he lit one up.

Outside my hotel, the river is full.
Crew teams force blades against water.

I'm alone to pack except on pavement
the Corona tracks my scent

back through the Gardens, riding my bumper until
the engine shuts down at the Long Island Sound.

The Gift
—*in a dream*

In my father's outstretched hands, a porgy,
dark side bars, well above the one-pound limit.

*But you shouldn't have done it. I'm too old
for gifts,* my child-voice says
at the edge of the Long Island Sound.

On driftwood, he splays that porgy into an arch.
Pins the sharp spines

into a stiff headdress.
Like a fisherman on a bamboo raft,
he dabs ink over flesh, freshly soaked.

Stuffs paper under slits. Blood seeps,
protruding lips, as if, as if
to tell me the meaning of such gifts.

A father's gift is a daughter's catch.
What do I do next, Father?

Under a waxing gibbous moon,
I Q-tip the porgy's eye dry.

Snow Falls

Crystals of frozen water fling
snow bombs over streets, cars and yards.
               At the Atlantic's decree,
snow buries Medford, Port Jeff. Now you sit
hot-glued to the club chair
as snow grows into the shoes of a nor'easter.

Remember when snow was all glitter and eggshells,
when your hands cared about weather,
or whether the deer family was steadied?

Remember the family yard sale. Next to the champagne splits,
your snow globes—thirty worlds

like eggs over easy Saturdays. That Saturday,
you bought your snow globes back. That night,

snowflakes called out as if they were children—
               Break the glass
where rosebuds nestled so close to the hammer.

As snow mounts, it's hard to remember:
nor'easters are only children of wind.

Now your hands hold onto what's saved,
or bury relics in land.fill – where you have a permit,

or grind what's left to dust like snow
unburdened when the Sound warms air.

Tender Trading

The dollar. The lira. Hues of green or red or blue. Stamped by presses.
Dead men's faces. Folded in wallets, crumpled in pockets,
hidden like Auntie's amethyst brooch or a tear caught in the throat.

Trade paper for paper. Numbers peek behind the seal.
Coins weighed like purple grapes. In piazzas. On street corners.
Paper for yellow tomatoes, wild fennel at Jefferson Market,

Antico Sosta. Two men push a wheelbarrow to a red truck. Six lambs.
Ankles tied. A metal arm lowers the scale, the hook,
hoist the lambs. Another and another. Hanging upside down.

Urine in the dirt. Under the arch,
men slap each other's backs with liras.
Carmine Street. The butcher.

Trading dollars for lambs hung from cords,
guts tied inside a rib cage,
freshly skinned.

Pipe's Cove

Chill stitches the undercoat.
Father cannot lift the boat onto icy logs.

The tide turns back. Blue-lipped, I
twist my mouth. The village is swollen

with daybreak. Footprints
over the path, where bamboo bends

snow-laden. The ashen bay rolls over
a rim of glass, salt-crusted over

open mouthed razor clams
orphaned by the heat of a morning star.

To the Sound

Behind me Shakespeare's *furlongs of sea*,
the land of whin, ill health, gorse
with drowned yellow flowers.

Wearing barnacle medals,
my gait over slick stones,
Sound greets me without asking.

Seadog songs unravel
as I sit at Sound's feet
   shush-sha-shush-
waves against my breasts
where Sound is knocking,
a hollow worn smooth
   shush-sha-shush-
on a quilt of tidal pool light.

When tides race east,
sun showers the oyster reef.
Westerly currents and rain.
To know the Sound for certain,
my brow smooth as a beach stone.

Sea lace umbrellas cuttlefish,
their calcified hearts. Sound holds parasols
and plunder and still stays Sound!

Home now. My porch is wide enough,
drenched in light. My couch.
One-woman deep. Whaling ballad:

Wide-Light-Deep. Wharf swans
hide behind each other, glide into one.

Blanket of sand, I kneel upon,
hand over hand,

until the night boat tolls,
until dusk unfolds her haze-gray cape.

Vivian Eyre lives in Southold, NY, a whisper's distance from the Long Island Sound. Her poems have appeared in many literary journals, including *Asheville Poetry Review, Bellingham Review, FRiGG, Green Hills Literary Lantern, Limestone Journal, Oberon, Permafrost, Quiddity, Sanskrit* and *Spoon River Poetry Review.* Vivian was a finalist for the Dorothy Daniels Award (2004), and a semi-finalist for *Calyx*'s Lois Cranston Memorial Poetry Prize (2011). *The Bellingham Review* nominated Vivian for the anthology, *Best New Poets 2013.* Vivian judges the North Fork's annual student Poetry for Peace Project and leads poetry workshops in recreation centers, libraries and at the Southold Free library. A leadership coach, Vivian has taught career workshops for women at Cornell University's ILR School, Harvard's Workplace Center and MIT.

PL G
014-

PORTLAND PUBLIC LIBRARY SYSTEM
5 MONUMENT SQUARE
PORTLAND, ME 04101